Hello, Baby

by Glen Franklin and Sue Bodman

illustrated by Laura Watson

'Hello, Baby,' says Mum.

Baby cries.

3

'Hello, Baby,' says Dad.

Baby cries.

'Hello, Baby,' says Gran.

Baby cries.

'Hello, Baby,' says Teddy.

Baby cries.

'Hello, Baby,' says Ben.

Baby cries.

'Hello, Baby,' says Sam.

Baby cries.

'Hello, Baby,' says Grandad.

Baby smiles.

Hello, Baby ✦ Glen Franklin and Sue Bodman

Teaching notes written by Sue Bodman and Glen Franklin

Using this book

Developing reading comprehension

Everyone tries to stop Baby crying. Even Teddy can't help. It takes Grandad's arrival to make Baby smile. Two short sentence patterns are repeated on every page, narrating how each member of the family tries to make baby smile. The verb changes on the final page.

Grammar and sentence structure

- Text is well spaced to support the development of one-to-one correspondence.

- Two lines of text reinforce return sweep onto a new line of text.

- The use of the present tense throughout (i.e. use of *'cries'*, *'says'* and *'smiles'*) gives the story an immediacy.

Word meaning and spelling

- Check vocabulary predictions by looking at the first letter of each character's names *(Mum, Dad, Gran, Grandad)*.

- Rehearse blending easy to hear sounds into a simple name *Sam Ben*.

- Use of capital letters for names.

Curriculum links

Language Development – Ask the children to bring in their baby pictures. Each child can tell the rest of the class what made them laugh or smile when they were a baby.

Drama – Facial expressions are an important method of social communication. Ask the children to work in pairs and enact a target emotion – happy, sad, angry, surprise. For slightly older children, more subtle emotions could be included – boredom, disgust, pride.

Learning Outcomes

Children can:

- understand that print carries meaning and is read from left to right, top to bottom

- read some high-frequency words

- use phonic knowledge to decode simple words.

A guided reading lesson

Introducing the text

Give a book to each child and read the title.

Orientation

Give a brief orientation to the text: *In this story, Baby cries. She cries and cries. Her family try and make her happy. But still she cries. I wonder why? Let's find out.*

Preparation

Page 2: *'Hello, Baby' says Mum.'* Find the words on the page *'Hello, Baby'*. Think about the sounds you can hear at the beginning of each word. *'Hello.' ' Baby'*. Support the children to hear the initial sound of these words and locate them on the page.

Then ask the children to notice the word *'Baby'* on the next line: *I can see the word 'Baby' on the next line. Can you find the two places where the word 'Baby' is on this page?* Support if necessary.

Model reading the text, pointing to each word as you read. Then ask the children to practise, checking that they are tracking word to word, matching the speed of the finger movement with the pace of reading.

Page 4: *Who comes in next to try and make Baby smile? Look at the picture – who might come in after Mum? You think it's Dad. Check the writing. Let's read – 'Hello Baby,*